T0065364

The Lion and The Lamb Within

A Poetic Expression of Love and Faith

JAMIE ANN COLANGELO

WESTBOW
PRESS®
A DIVISION OF THOMAS NELSON
& ZONDERVAN

WestBow Press books may be ordered through booksellers or by contacting:

WestBow Press
A Division of Thomas Nelson & Zondervan
1663 Liberty Drive
Bloomington, IN 47403
www.westbowpress.com
844-714-3454

Because of the dynamic nature of the Internet, any web addresses or
links contained in this book may have changed since publication and
may no longer be valid. The views expressed in this work are solely those
of the author and do not necessarily reflect the views of the publisher,
and the publisher hereby disclaims any responsibility for them.

Any people depicted in stock imagery provided by Getty Images are
models, and such images are being used for illustrative purposes only.
Certain stock imagery © Getty Images.

Scriptures taken from the Holy Bible, New International Version®, NIV®.
Copyright © 1973, 1978, 1984, 2011 by Biblica, Inc.™ Used by permission
of Zondervan. All rights reserved worldwide. www.zondervan.com The
"NIV" and "New International Version" are trademarks registered in
the United States Patent and Trademark Office by Biblica, Inc.®

ISBN: 978-1-6642-1895-6 (sc)
ISBN: 978-1-6642-1894-9 (e)

Print information available on the last page.

WestBow Press rev. date: 2/3/2021

TO:

FROM:

Dedication

I dedicate this book to my Lord
and Savior, Jesus Christ.
He is my ever present help
and the Lover of my soul.

Acknowledgements

I give thanks to God for His love and faithfulness. He has given me the gift of poetry to express myself and His love through me.

I am grateful for His provision through others and their gifts that have made this book possible.

Thank you to Samantha Tetro for giving our poetry group a home. It is a safe, welcoming place where we can come together and express our faith in the poetry we create. We support one another on our individual journeys while encouraging and sharing with each other the gifts the Lord has bestowed upon us.

Thank you to Linda Trott Dickman and James P. Wagner for your passion for poetry and willingness to invest in our group. Your kindness, time, keen eye and ear to hear, has blessed me tremendously. Thank you both, as well, for opening up other doors to share my poetry and the love of the Lord.

Thank you to Linda Trott Dickman for continuing to facilitate the group. And a special thank you for your interest and time invested in coming alongside me and getting this book on its way.

Thank you to family and friends, who have encouraged me, enjoyed and shared my poems.

Thank you to the publishing team for their expertise and for helping me through this process.

Thank you to all who lifted me up in prayer.

I appreciate all of you. May God bless you and your families.

Foreword

The "Lion and The Lamb Within" literally left me breathless. Poet Jamie Ann's ability to paint a picture with her words engages the heart of the reader from page one!

Similar to a modern day version of The Psalms, the author gently leads you on an emotional journey of comfort and calm, anguish and angst, fear and faith.

Join her as she slowly unveils the love, joys, hurts and hopes of what we call "LIFE".

Don't rush through it though. Sit . Reflect. Savor . Pray. Praise.

The turning of each page unwraps a gift of a poem filled with such emotion and transparency that one no longer sees the author but themselves.

As we "see" ourselves, you will also see your need for a Savior. For He truly is the lover of your soul and the lifter of your head. Healing and hope awaits you! The "Lion and The Lamb Within" is a life changer for sure!

Samantha Tetro

Samantha's "Li'l Bit of Heaven Ministries"

Foreword

Jamie Ann Colangelo's latest book, *The Lion and The Lamb Within,* is a faith filled journey through the complex situations and moments that make up a life. Jamie Ann beckons us to Wake up in the first poem, and we are off to experience joy, pain, loss, recovery, clouds and their silver linings. If ever there was a time for encouragement, it is now, and *The Lion and The Lamb Within,* is a faithful testimony to the light that remains faithful in the darkest times.

Linda Trott Dickman

Introduction

The poems in this book were created during extremely difficult times. The marital strife, abandonment, rejection and depression were more than enough. But then there was the breast cancer, the slow and unexplained difficulty healing, and the painful side effects of treatment and medication, along with other health issues and chronic pain from injuries sustained earlier in life. I didn't think I could handle anymore nor think my heart could break anymore. Yet it did, when my son suffered a debilitating illness. I thought I had already cried every tear, but no, so many, many, more followed. And then Covid19 struck.

While I had no control, I continued praying and seeking God for His wisdom, strength, and grace. I leaned in, trusting Him for all my needs and those of my family. There is so much that I do not understand. Yet, I know that my God is a God of love and goodness. He is faithful, He is with me, and He will continue to take me through.

I pray that these poems will bless you and encourage you. And may the Lord draw you even closer to Himself.

To God be the glory.

Jamie Ann Colangelo

Numbers 6:24-26 New International Version (NIV)

²⁴ """The LORD bless you
  and keep you;
²⁵ the LORD make his face shine on you
  and be gracious to you;
²⁶ the LORD turn his face toward you
  and give you peace."'

Contents

Rise Up – Shine Your Light

Wake Up, Wake up

My precious child
Open up your sleepy eyes
It's time to rise
It's time to shine

Look all around you
Hearts are hard
And love's gone cold
The world's grown dark

Get up and Go
And be the light
You are the brilliance
In this hopeless world

Where is My Faith?

Is my faith in people?
Or is it in my job?
In the money I've saved?
Or the things I've stored?

People will disappoint
My job may be lost
Savings may be depleted
And stored things, exhausted

My faith is in the One
Who first gave it to me
A small measure
A huge treasure

Yes - He is the One
Inexhaustible
Never ending supply
His name - Is Jesus

The Precious Blood

Jesus

Precious blood shed
To raise us from the dead
For sin had taken its toll
On each and every soul
A Father's love so great
His Son would meet His fate
As He hung upon the cross
To save the loved but lost

Jesus

Shipwrecked

S-Stay
H-Hopeful
I-In
P-Prayer
W-With
R-Righteousness
E-Enveloped in
C-Christ
K-King
E-Eternally
D-Divine

My God, My Strong Tower

It was a beautiful day
Without a cloud in the sky
My sight extends far away
My spirit leaps to new highs

Suddenly, without warning
Shrouded in a cloud cover
A perfect storm was brewing
Ominous waves hover

The water bears down on me
Salty splashes burn my eyes
Vision gone, I cannot see
Will this - this - be my demise?

My heart's pounding, gripped by fear
Fiercely trembling, I cower
"Oh My God, My God, come near,
Gird me in Your strong tower"

Isolation - Spending Time with the Lord

I-Inside and all alone
S-Set apart for the Lord
O-Opening my eyes and ears
L-Listening for His voice
A-Adoring Him more and more
T-Treasuring His Presence
I-Intent on following Him
O-Offering myself as a living sacrifice
N-No turning back – Welcoming the New Season

Love From Above

A fresh breath of life
Lifting up, giving hope
A word of warning
Correction, redirection
A gentle kiss from Our God
Expressing His affection

One in Him

Set apart in this pandemic lockdown
Wading through endless hours alone
Waves of worries surround
Battling fear of the unknown

Darkness looms, crying out
I need a word, Your touch
Lord, what is this all about?
Covid19, poverty, separation-too much!

Set apart for the work to be done
Going through, growing through
Each, maturing and becoming one
Holding on to the One that is true

Standing on the Rock, Who is Love
An army rising up, no longer mute
Expecting miracles from above
And- an abundance of fruit!

The Good News is What I Choose

I thought about the news
Decided not to tune in
Listening to it infrequently
Something that I choose
Rarely does it uplift
Often filled with gore and fear
Instead I open to scripture
To focus on the good news
It reminds me that I'm secure
Keeps my eyes on God
Only then, can I walk on water

When Love Is Real

Many think that Love...
is the feeling of butterflies in their belly
or the rush that makes their face flush
or the obsession occupying their mind

Some say that Love...
is a contract, binding, yet
breakable when one person
does not fulfill their part

But Love...
"Love, I say will become real
when brought to the altar"
because Love is a covenant

Love stands, Love fights,
Love gives, Love forgives,
Love perseveres when all else fails
because Love... Never fails

Mary, Chosen Maiden, Mother of God

She said "Yes" – Will You?

She was just a child
Perhaps early teens
Recently betrothed
A choice made for her

An angel met her
On a normal day
Bearing a message
Far from the normal

The Holy Spirit
Would come upon her
For she was chosen
To carry God's Son

Blessed, highly favored
Pregnant on a mule
Running for her life
And for her unborn

Trusting in the man
Who wanted divorce
Upon hearing news
That she was with child

Led by her husband
Through dreams in the night
For a place to birth
God's begotten Son

Outside the filled Inn
Inside the stable
Bearing down in pain
The Savior was born

The simple maiden
Surrendered her will
To deliver Him
Who'd deliver us

Caring for her boy
As a loving mom
Until that dark day
That her heart was pierced

Kneeling at the cross
Cries of agony
Tears drenching her clothes
Watching her son die

Her innocent yes
Trusting in her God
Brought life to Jesus
And hope to the world

Will you answer yes
Accepting Jesus
And carry Him to
A lost, dying world

The Kiss, The Embrace, The Problem

Man's Problem - God's Solution

The time had come
seated around the table
enjoying their last meal
the bread - dipped in wine
The command was issued
do what you must
and do it quickly
He rose up and went
then the kiss, the embrace
the problem, betraying
the One sentenced to death
A fulfillment of scripture
with the heart of the Father
that none should perish
if they believed in His Son
For the death before us
exchanged for eternal life
through a problem
delivered through man
turned into a solution
delivered through God

One Solitary Seed

New Life - Out of darkness and into the light

One solitary seed
Buried deep within the earth
Cold, hard, and lifeless,
Trampled over and over
Drenched by unceasing rain

Suddenly, cracked open
And released from its tomb
Springing forth new life
Bearing abundant fruit
For all who will receive

The blessing, hidden
In the depths of darkness
Now beams the greatest light
One solitary seed

Dearest Mother

Lovingly dedicated to My Mom

You were a dear, loving mother
Imperfect, moody, tough, gentle
All the facets of who you were
Cut in the trials you endured

Battling through in the darkest night
Brilliantly revealed in the light
A warrior, overcoming
Obstacles sent to defeat you

Your heart tried, tested and refined
Filled with love, wisdom, compassion
Looking for the best and grateful
For what is, trusting this will pass

Moving you onward and hopeful
Pressing forward to better days
The strength, courage, exemplified
The faith and trust God placed in you

So Much of the Sweetness

In Life Comes From Family

The walls that surround me here
Could tell a tale or two
The times we had to share
And memories – more than a few

For every passing year
Was filled with laughter
Joy, sorrow and tears
Times, I reminisce, days after

Moments that I treasure
Etched upon my heart
Love beyond measure
Never to be apart

My family's grown and gone
From the walls that surround me here
But the memories live on
Held always to me dear

I Would Die For...

I would die for my son
I would die for my daughter
I would die for the One
Who was led to the slaughter

A life freely given
A sacrifice of great cost
That we may be forgiven
Redeemed, and no longer lost

I would pick up my cross
And press on to the finish
Because I understand the loss
If I choose to be selfish

Others may not see it
And choose their own thrill
But my choice is to be in it
Empowered by God's will

His Light, His Son in You

Every Cloud Has a Silver Lining

So it is said
Every cloud has a silver lining
The hope of which
The sun, hidden
Behind, in time
Breaks through its light
Biblically,
It is pure joy
Tribulations
Trials, sorrows
Testing your faith
Perseverance
Produced in you
Having its way
Working for good
Maturing and
Yielding you to
The Refiners'
Fire, burning away
All that's hidden
Darkness within
His Light breaks through
Revealing His Son
In you, through you

My Transformation

The unending stream of tears
The pain, anguish, and fears
Consuming, paralyzing a good life
Following news, you no longer wanted a wife

Delivered swiftly with one phone call
Carelessly, recklessly abandoning all
A dream, a hope, and a plan
Thwarted by a decision of a man

Desperately trying to breathe
Haunted by the nightmares of the eve
Wanting to end this emotional pain
Thinking of ways, totally insane

The precious family I loved dearly
Seeking to protect and fight fearlessly
Holding on, relinquishing it all
To the only One I could call

My King, My Lord, My Savior
And the Lover of my soul
Embraced by His strong and loving arms
My future, my family, held in His palms

Then it came
I'd never be the same
The revelation
About my transformation

Called to rise up and to stand
Against powers that befallen this land
A family hanging in the balance
The lies, the deception, holding them captive

Using the gifts and talents given to me
To war against the enemy
Co-laboring with Jesus, my Lord
A princess warrior for the One who is my reward

Lifting Him up in worship for all to see
Giving Him glory, reclaiming territory
Hoping to bring others into the fold
That they may one day walk on streets of gold

Today, I can face adversity
For I know with Whom I will spend eternity

Turn My Anger Into Righteousness

The beauty of my being
Like a Dieffenbachia
Set in an earthen clay pot
Adorned with silver and gold
Broadly expressing myself
Variating shades throughout
Of glossy greens and yellows
Brilliantly kept at its best
And thriving with gentle care
Attentive watering, warmth,
Low, medium or bright light

Revealing my inmost parts
Honestly, authentically
To the core, believing in
A heart and an ear to hear
Only to be blindsided
By the reaction displayed
Cutting me down - One swoop
Closing my throat, shutting down,
Suffocating in likeness
To the toxic sap within
Speechless, I sat and remained

Crying out to God for help
For understanding, wisdom
Healing for my broken heart
Wondering why my requests
Fell again on a deaf ear
Instead of the wide open

Elephant Ear, ready and
Attuned to hear without fear
But, Dumb Cane, chose to murder
Burning my skin and killing
The gentle spirit within

Crying out again to God
Take this pain away from me
Help me to let go, forgive
Let no bitter root grow nor
Offense take my life from me
Water me with Your pure love
Restoring me and working
Everything out for my good
Raising me up tall and proud
To the oak of righteousness
You have designed me to be

Good at Nothing

This is dedicated to the One I Love Who Loved Me First

Good-no-i am not
Good at anything
No God-i'm nothing
He has given me
Eyes, ears and a mouth
To see, hear, and speak
To be who He called
Me to be, chosen
For His purposes
The gifts and talents
And breath for today
Radiating Him
His love and kindness
Broken and poured out
To a dying world
Desperate for hope
His mercy and grace
Ev'rything in me
Given for one, all
Bestowing glory
To our Lord, Savior
So none would perish
And He shall receive
The inheritance
For the life He gave

Forgiven - Redeemed

You are My precious princess
My multifaceted diamond
With every cut My love shines through
Revealing all of Me in you

The price I paid was worth it
My sacrifice of love is to forgive
My death - to give you life
And redeem you as My wife

Heaven's Embrace

Effortlessly floating
Supported only by
The unseen crevices
Of the still atmosphere

She's lovingly embraced
And Illuminated
By the radiant glow
That fills the sky above

Drifting ever downward
Held by heaven above
By a cord umbilic
From Father's heart to hers

The Ghost in The House

Invited in, welcomed
To take inventory
Seeing the good in me
And the not so good too

Holy Ghost convicts me
To work out salvation
Removing all the flaws
Left by sin and trauma

Restoring my house back
To Your original
Unique design for me
By the blood of Your Son

Jesus, Whose righteousness
Covered me, His spirit
Lives within all my days
From the day I said *Yes*

The Ghost in The House

The River of Renewal

The River of Renewal
Runs through my veins
Rushing, flushing,
Away every stain

The River of Renewal
Runs through my veins
Coursing, forcing,
Out every hindrance

The River of Renewal
Runs through my veins
Streaming, steeping,
Every weary cell

The River of Renewal
Runs through my veins
Surging, soaking,
Every parched fiber

The River of Renewal
Filters, distills,
Quenches, instills,
New life to being

Your Breath in Me

The gentle rhythm
Rising up and down
Infilling my lungs
Oxygenating
Precious blood flowing
Through my arteries
Delivering life
Throughout my body
It is Your *ruach*
Your Holy Spirit
Your power moving
In me and through me
It's Your breath in me

Don't Stop Until You're Proud

Battling, battling, battling
Over and over in my head
Voices, voices, voices
Telling me my dreams are dead

Trusting, trusting, trusting
Resurrection reversed the fall
Pressing, pressing, pressing
On and on to the upward call

Believing, believing, believing
He has great plans for me
Rejoicing, rejoicing, rejoicing
In the One who holds my destiny

Listening, listening, listening
To His voice, in stillness, made loud
Don't stop, don't stop, don't stop
Your Heavenly Father is proud

Called to Arms in the Dark of Night

In the dark of night
I am fast asleep
All's quiet and right
Not even a peep
Can be heard within
Nor be heard without
I am surrendered
Completely at ease
My heart is rendered
Ready to receive
The dreams and visions
Providing wisdom
Direction, knowledge
For myself, others
Awakened to pray
Entering the war
Battling for the Lord
Those upon His heart
Trusting the power
And authority
Bestowed upon me
By the finished work
At Calvary's cross
Declaring it's done
The battle's been won
In the heavenlies
And upon this earth
According to Him
Above and below

I Am The Message In The Bottle

Cut down and crushed
Battered, beaten to a pulp
Squeezed, dried, stretched
Bleached white and branded
Every fiber indelibly marked
Placed inside and set adrift
Day and night, braving
Hot blazing sun, cold crushing waves
Tossing, turning, tumbling
Wondering when the time will come
To release the voice inside this vessel
I am the message in the bottle

Judah Roared Back

It was the county clerk
Riverhead location
My husband, like clockwork
Squashed my devotion
To my Lord and Savior
Judah rose up in me
And roared for God's favor
That I would hear and see
Big and bold, loud and clear
After many delays
The tall man, sent to bear
Witness, declared His ways
Pointing to me, he said,
"Jesus loves you", smiling,
"God bless you" I declared
My husband, now smiling,
Said "Right up your alley"

And so it was, Judah
Mirroring back to me
Alive and glorified
For all to hear and see

Jesus Met and Set Us Free In A Locksmith Shop

Standing over 6 feet the day I met you
Intimidated by your incredibly inked arms
Unintentionally eavesdropping
My heart awakened with compassion
Upon hearing the anguish in your voice

Nervously waiting to pray for you
Debating if I should or shouldn't
Concerned you'd think I'm weird
Conflicted - arguing with Jesus
Reminded - I said I'd be weird

As you started up the steps
My inquiry about your affliction
Proceeded from trembling lips
A response of a foot malady, I'd never heard
I asked you if you knew Jesus

A welcome response you supplied
And an offer to pray for you
Graciously and gratefully accepted
With a comment that you'd been praying
And no answer was coming-Then you stopped

Could it possibly be
That the Lord spoke to you
That He had sent me
To answer the fervent prayers
Of a righteous man?

Seated upon a wooden bench
In a typical locksmith shop
You – Jose', waited eagerly
To receive the prayers of healing
From the agony that had you gripped

Kneeling down on the dirty floor
Contrasted to my all white apparel
My hands met your flip-flopped foot
Thanking the Lord for you, your heart for Him
Thanking Him for releasing the healing

His blessings poured out upon you
That ordinary summer day
And upon me as well
As I answered His call to rise up
And deliver the extraordinary to you

Embraced By Glory

Sitting seaside, surrounded
by natures' wonders
Waves crest and fall
ushering in a melody
of sand and surf

Misty sea breezes caress
my face, depositing wet kisses
upon my blushing cheeks
Salt air fills my nostrils as
the sun, rising, warms my skin

Rays sprinkle upon the waters
glistening, reflecting back
into the atmosphere
The sky is set aglow
yellows, oranges, reds

The breaking dawn
envelops me in her peace
undisturbed by the
busyness of the world
still, yet asleep

A moment of time
captured in stillness
Embraced by glory

Heaven Has a Dock

Heaven has a dock
It's my favorite place to go
There's no watching of a clock
Just the gentle waters flow

Surrounded by His peace
The warmth of the sun
Dancing rays of light
Creation stuns the Holy One

The scent of salted air
The breeze upon my neck
His touch runs through my hair
As I sit upon the deck

Drifting off to sleep
As the tide gently rocks
Cradled by His love
Here on Heaven's dock

Autumn Blessings

Standing lakeside - Alone
Yet, embraced by all that surrounds
Listening intently to the sounds
The deafening sounds of silence
My lungs fill with crisp fall air
Refreshing, reenergizing, reawakening
Like my taste buds at first bite
Of a freshly picked apple

Gazing upward, brilliant blue sky
Rays of sun, warmly kissing my face
Trees standing at attention
Bejeweled by ever changing leaves
Like garland streaming from heaven
Each one uniquely, brilliantly
Expressing its colors

Below, calm, crystal water
Perfectly reflecting their majesty
Meditating on the Creator
His creation and who He created us to be
Fearfully, wonderfully made
Reflecting His magnificence
In His image - All for His glory!

He Is Holding You in His Hand

Fervently- I prayed the day you came home
Hopes held high that you would decide to stay
You yelled - You cursed - You wanted to be alone
Your anger and harsh words pushed me away

Off you went without a kiss or goodbye
Running wherever- I have not a clue
Questions- over and over as to why
This mental breakdown has come upon you

You seemed determined on cutting the ties
Swiftly heading in a strange direction
While I wonder why you believed the lies
I hold on for a restored connection

My faith in God, our Creator, I stand
Trusting- He is holding you in His hand

On Abba Father's Heart

She had a vivid dream
To her, extremely weird
A message meant for me
I'm remembered, endeared
God sees the liquid prayers
He hears my hopeless cries
Her dream, many layers
Revealed to seeking eyes
For those that are hidden
Invisible, they're not
Every name is written
On Abba Father's Heart

The Woman He Sees In Me

A dialogue between mirrors

The woman in the looking glass
broken, scarred, hopeless
covered in dirt, in poverty
orphaned, desperate
Is the one looking back at me

A dialogue between mirrors
tells a new story
the woman in the looking glass
made Whole, healed, hopeful
covered in blood, in abundance
adopted, joyful
Is the one Jesus sees in me

The Savior's Love for Me

My precious daughter
Oh how I love you
With an everlasting heart
One you cannot fathom
You are so beautiful in My sight
The sparkling of your eyes
Brighter than the stars at night
Your hair is softer than silk
Your teeth, whiter than milk
You are My sunshine
And the apple of My eye

Even through your tear stained face
Your radiance shines through
You doubt this love I have for you
The many trials you have been through
Have left you weary and discouraged
But in the sorrows, I have been with you
I have felt your pain and given you courage
Your tears were not in vain My dear
Trust in Me and you will persevere
My love for you is true
My life, I gave for you

My Princess – My Bride

You've dreamed of the days to come
Waiting and waiting for that special One
The One who would lift you up above
The One who would give you all His love

In the abuse, abandonment and rejection
In the depths of heartbreak, you chose to be My reflection
Rise up, My dear, your time has come
Leave the cinders behind, My precious one
Your Creator, Lover of your soul, makes all things new
Beauty for ashes, I bestow upon you

Washed clean and clothed in My royalty
Princess slippers and a crown for all to see
In your hand, I place the Kingdom's key
And together, we will dance, through all eternity

The Golden Gate

High above the deepest blue
Magnificent, breathtaking, is the view
The great expanse beckons me
To follow through to where I cannot see
I leave familiar chains behind
Aroused and eager for what I may find
I trust in the One who led me here
Crossover and do not fear
This journey has been done in faith
Promised Land found, through the Golden Gate

Open Territory

Arriving at a canvas of pure white
I am awed by the expanse
Of all that lies before me
Territory, open and undefined
Waiting for me and my creativity
To choose boldly all that is within
And to fearlessly step in
Courageously saying "yes"
To all the Lord has promised
Envisioning a life, abundant,
Vivid and bejeweled
In a spectrum of colors
Painting my future
Amazing, Beautiful, Magnificent

Afterword

Thank you for taking the time to read and savor the poems in this book. I pray and believe that our Heavenly Father has touched your heart in a very special way.

For those who have already asked Jesus into their hearts, I pray that He draws you even closer in intimacy with Him.

For those who have not yet asked Jesus into their hearts and would like to, you can say the following prayer.

Heavenly Father, I come to You from the depths of my heart and confess that I am a sinner. I repent of my sins and confess that Jesus Christ is the Son of God and died on the cross for me and my sins. I believe You raised Him from the dead.

I ask You, Lord Jesus, to come into my heart. I receive You as my Lord and Savior. I receive Your Holy Spirit as my Comforter. Help me to obey You and do Your will. In Jesus name, I pray. Amen.

Romans 10:9-10 New International Version (NIV)

[9] If you declare with your mouth, "Jesus is Lord," and believe in your heart that God raised him from the dead, you will be saved. [10] For it is with your heart that you believe and are justified, and it is with your mouth that you profess your faith and are saved.

About the Author

Jamie Ann Colangelo is a Christian, living on Long Island. She is the mother of twins, Liane and Christopher, now adults. She is the author of From The Father's Heart - A Book of Poems and Suggested Gifts To Inspire, Encourage and Bless Those in Your Circle of Influence. She found her passion for poetry at the age of 12 and now enjoys using her gifts and talents to share God's love and encourage others on life's journey.

Printed in the United States
By Bookmasters